Triple No. 12

Meg Pokrass
Angela Readman
Jeff Alessandrelli

The Ravenna Triple Series

Chapbooks as they were meant to be read—
in good company.

ISBN: 978-1-7351131-8-0

Published by Ravenna Press
USA
ravennapress.com

FIRST EDITION

Meg Pokrass

An Object at Rest

For Philip

Contents

An Object at Rest

"Rain comes from holes in the clouds," Dad said. "Don't be annoyed with it. Respect it," he said. I tried to think about holes in the clouds, like mouseholes or else, moth holes in my sweaters. My sweaters were full of mysterious little rips these days. We were driving to my dance lesson and I was tired of the rain ruining everything. I was tired of the hole in our house since Mom died, how things were still unravelling, and I hated the way he drove me to my ballet class just late enough that I'd slump in right after it began. The teacher would look at me and smile because she was good at conveying pity. The rumor about her was that her dancing toes stopped curling or pointing when she was in her late 20s, a professional dancer in New York. That she tried to commit suicide.

"Just look at her wrists," Dad said, when he signed me up for her expensive class. "They're always covered".

"How do you know?" I asked. He smiled and lit a clove cigarette.

"And here's something else to keep in mind. Clouds rip because they are made of cotton, or wool, and sometimes they're made from smoke, like some people's dreams," Dad said. I tried to imagine my dance teacher in a leotard, leaping around a stage with other dancers, young and ambitious.

Sometimes Dad said that he too was going to learn to dance. This worried and amused me.

"An object at rest has no energy," he sighed. He rested so often that he seemed more and more like an old man, a person whose time had passed.

"Well then," I said, "it's time to kick the world in the ass." But I didn't mean it. The thought of him dancing made me want to stop.

These were the kinds of things I could hear myself trying not to think about with my father, the two of us sitting next to each other on the sofa together watching game shows every weekend. Well-wishers were long gone, the pity and nosy excitement from the neighbors after my mother's death slipping away, just as her love had.

I tried to imagine other still creatures, the energy being drained from their faces. All I could think about was a rattle snake I'd seen crossing the road when Mom and I were on our way to dance class the month before she died. How she stopped the car and we just sat there watching the snake slither stupidly across the busy road. "Shall we let it live?" she asked me. "Yes, yes!" I said. But that was before I knew it who would hurt me. That I'd trip over a snake just trying to forget all of what my father had untaught me.

"Do you remember what you used to announce to me and your Momma?" Dad asked me. "How you insisted that the earth was shaped like a pancake?"

"We're almost there, Dad," I said. I begged him to pull over to the curb. I could get out and walk the rest of the way in my ballet slippers. I could be late because of my own doing, for once.

That time, he let me. I took my time, sitting on the curb, pulling the scabs off my sweater, poking at the holes in my tights. Trying to imagine luckier mothers driving past, looking at snakes with endangered faces, letting them live.

Worries of the Duck

She wishes he were more like the females. He appears like all the other shiny males lying at the lake by day, staring blankly at the sun, dunking his perfect head. At midnight he moans miserably about the turning moon—worries the way tortoises do. Near a long, fallen branch in the shallow spot she sits on their eggs, urgent and large. He comes and goes all day and night with fancy, fanned-out wings—touching the nest, swimming away.

Greetings From Mars

"Greetings from Mars," I write on five postcards from the insane hotel we're staying in. My son rolls around on the planetary carpet, singing in a high-pitched voice, trying to make me laugh.

We've been partying all night. "Mom, that Russian slot machine has your name on it," he says.

When we checked in, the front desk clerk asked me about my married status. "You need to check it in the box right here," she said. "Married, Divorced, Single."

I could feel my son's mood heating up next to me. Could feel his face redden. "Fuck this," he said.

"My husband died a few weeks ago," I explained.

"Whoa. Okay. Then, 'widow' is what you should say. You can just write that in."

*

But Vegas itself is infectious. Nothing as it seems. I can laugh while drizzling rain from my eyes.

"Mom, we're having a ball here," my son admits, and it's true. He's a year too young but I share beer with him and let him choose which dumb outfit I'll wear to the Stratosphere.

The Hawaiian shirt he's wearing is the one Bob gave him for middle school graduation. Our son smiled that day with bee-stinger confidence. Now he doesn't match the decor.

*

In the Orbit Cafe at noon, there's a lot to love. Our waitress's tentacle hair, gravity toast that floats, seeing my son with his moon-glow eyes and a sunrise smile Bob would have ordered up.

I recall our honeymoon here in Vegas.

How I lay on my back, knees in the air. "I'm cooking up our kid."

"Stick a pin in that thought," Bob said, shuffling into the bathroom which resembled a space capsule.

I pretend he's in there now. Close my eyes and watch myself hover over Earth. After all, we've landed here again. When I close my eyes, we're about to win.

Wonderful Dog

When her husband came home, the three of them would snuggle on the sofa and he would tell her about other dogs on other shores. He'd show her the glint of moonlight on his heart. Would tell her how none of the dogs before this one were smart enough, funny enough. How he had been waiting for an animal to love him exactly this way.

"Here you are," he'd say. "You and this wonderful dog."

He would tell her about the fungus growing inside his soul, how it ate his words up too. It wasn't that he didn't trust her, didn't love her.

The dog would understand this completely.

The man would sit on the floor as if he were part of a dog family. She'd throw them the ball and one of them or both of them would bring it back.

Teeth

Heart pumping against my back, he said he wanted to be with me forever as though I would want to know it, but I could barely hear him over the barking of a dog down the block, some confused or tired dog—but I still loved him then because he would nod his head at sounds as though he really heard them, not the dumb things I said; would laugh as if the sound of my thoughts were just right.

Kissing him, I'd keep my eyes open. Those awful teeth I had in middle school, the ones they corrected— I felt them again. Every time. It was them being kissed, not me.

Married Hat

In the end, he sent back Sophia's hat. But in the beginning, it was her hat that Ed was drawn to. Her hat must have felt to him like a lighthouse. In the middle of a long, dark swim, it was her hat he seemed to be drawn to. Which is why she left it in his car on their last night together.

"Why do you live in seclusion with such a face, and such a hat?" He said at the coffee shop in Little Italy on their first outing. "It's my marriage," she said, as if she were saying "cancer".

"Well, then it's a privilege to be here with you, and your face, and your married hat," Ed said. And he stared at her inside her hat. His face, deeply unsatisfied. He had a sensual mouth.

Sophia was the youngest daughter of a woman who had given up on men. The daughter of a woman who had become a monk.

She wanted the smell of this man, the way his swimmer's wet voice touched the tips of her ears, the way his fat, unsatisfied mouth would melt right into hers.

Sophia, with her face, with her depressed husband who had stopped touching her, had so much desire. And here was Ed, sitting across from her now, smiling at her hat.

New Contortionist

I opened the door to the bite of cigarette stench, and there he was. My guy, my strong man with his boots untied, smoking next to the new contortionist, surrounded by a cloud of fuzzy poison. He looked at me as though he needed oxygen, but not mine.

The contortionist sucked on a joint, twiddled her toes and held her arms out as though she were balancing a nest of eggs. I imagined her toes long, flexible and good for keeping life still. Sienna-colored hair, the scent of flightless doves.

My strong man loved mermaids and tropical fish. Collected photographs of frisky female clowns. With his women, he fancied the kind who wore hip flasks and visited late at night with Absinthe breath.

Circus women are not supposed to be possessive. We're not tender, as a rule. He knew this and I knew this— so I just stood there feeling my toes curl under.

Frankenstein Worms

My husband woke me up with childlike excitement about the mysteries of life after death. “Hey, Hon. In Siberia, three-hundred prehistoric Roundworms have come back to life,” he said. “I read about it and just, felt good and I still feel that way, and the day is just starting.”

I turned over and tried to remember my dream. In the dream, I was living on a tropical island, floating on a raft, the water aquamarine blue. A sea gull landed on my head, and I didn’t mind. I said to the bird, “go ahead and shit on me again.”

But I couldn’t get back into the dream world, with my husband singing so loudly, it was impossible (from the sound of his baritone) to believe how cynical he was before we moved here. He sang in the kitchen, cooking white rice for our difficult stomachs, and reading about Frankenstein worms. It was a difficult prize, in a way, being married to a songbird.

“Death really is only the beginning after all. It's sorta similar to being asleep or at least in a cryosleep, everything shuts down to its bare minimal,” I could hear him explaining to our Siberian Forest Cat, Ulf. We adopted Ulf soon after moving to Barrow, the only place where my husband could find employment and the only place we could have a decent life, even though we lived in the dark. Sixty days of the year there is no light here at all. When moving with your guy to Arctic, item number one, adopt a cat.

It was dark as a tomb in the bedroom. Lack of natural light can create fatal health situations, we all accepted this and many of us spent our days basking under U.V. lights.

So I stood up and shouted, "Coffee! Can you please bring me a cuppa?" Coffee was the one thing I looked forward to in Barrow, it's too bad it happened so early in the day. This was one of the things I loved about marriage, the way one could train a husband to bring you coffee in bed, and if he didn't remember, how you could simply go back to sleep for the rest of your afternoon.

I slid off my wizard slippers and glanced at the clock. It was three-pm, not bad. Almost dinner time.

I curled back up on bed and felt a bit flat, curled up like a worm. Realizing that you no longer recognize the earth you are wiggling around on. Surviving on fish and ten dollar -per package Oreo cookies. Reading about prehistoric worms. Waking up as a worm but a million years later, now that was something to dream about.

Otters Don't Live Here Anymore

Jesus, Mary and Joseph, I've started to see otters again. They say otters don't live here anymore, but they certainly seem to visit. I saw one lying on its back, nearly a cripple, licking its foot, the day Katie moved in with her netted hat. She looked as if she was fresh from safari, protected from every known type of insect. Some hat, I thought. *What a woman!*

I was hoping for a neighbor who was just a bit less hinky, but we get what we get.

"No bugs here, this time of year," I said. "You can probably take off your net."

She smiled a buzzy little smile right at me. I could tell she thought I was coming on to her. We both stood there, between our dwellings, and stared at the tired-looking otter.

"That thing looks dead," I said. "But he's come here to greet you." You can stand outside around here and hear nothing but birds singing.

"I like to create lots of warm, colourful layers," she said. "I'll invite you over when I'm settled in."

My mother might have said *that one was born for the stage*. She enunciated beautifully. Her face made of map lines; neck and shoulders as if they'd been baked in the Sahara.

And I could tell from the way she looked at the otter, straight into his feverish eyes, she was open for business. The thing about otters, they're hungry animals. I thought *aw hell, here it comes.*

You Can't Take it With You

There is nothing to do when waiting for this silly date but to walk up and down the block, worrying about your appearance, clutching your handbag. Recently, your mother's caretaker said that you reminded her of actresses from the 1930s, Myrna Loy meets June Allison, she said, and you feel sick because you're just yourself, just the same, but this is how people have started to see you.

A mountain of time is creeping over you like a moon-shadow. You listened to 1930s jazz in your car on the way to the date. Ethel Waters and Bessie Smith. Accepting that you yourself prefer a warm time capsule—wondering if your date will snicker when he sees your vintage boots.

This is what you're thinking about when the man you recognize from the photo glides right past you, standing in front of the café where you're supposed to meet him. You feel drawn to him like a light, dazed as a flapping moth. Your wings are out, ready to be singed. He reminds you of your leading man, the one who left you for an ingénue.

But this time you watch it play in the theatre of your mind. How he'll gaze at you while you sip your Gin Rickey, as if sitting back in an art-house cinema, squinting at the screen. "You remind me of someone," he'll say with a polite school-boy smile.

Jennifers

Jennifers are always so confident. But this one is hungry. She pushes me away while she unzips my fly. Says "please pretend," as she takes me in her warm, smooth hand.

There is a ragged nail. And this is why I come back. I like the way she says *why not?*, then swirls her bitten claw over my dick lightly. We're so ill at ease after all of that, holding hands, wondering what to do with this rigid, coal-black evening.

"Happy Valley, this city we live in," I say. She looks me over the way a hawk will a mouse. It's still hard to believe, that she is really a Jennifer. One who doesn't want anything more than this, a kind of weekly wandering with me, not caring what comes next.

I don't tell her she reminds me of my grandmother, dead before I was born. A haunted beauty smiling out of picture frames at me, her useless, crushed-out grandson who can't save her.

Sometimes I'm already old. Standing next to this Jennifer or that one.

The Sting

The pale man who wanted to buy me glowed like a ragged moth. He wasn't teasing anymore, he was there when I walked into the lobby, only whiter and skinnier than I thought he'd be. He looked me over calmly, a retired businessman with nothing to loose. Squeezed me by the shoulders.

Goddamnit it's good to meet you, he said.

It's wonderful to meet you too, I said, shaking his bony hand.

And I meant it. He had the face of a bored child who had taken a stand against emotion. And yet, I felt I could make him laugh. Perhaps he simply needed a bit of watering once a year, like a cactus.

"My knees feel like resting," he said. And I realized that we'd been standing there frozen in time for more than a few minutes, not knowing what to do with our hands or our mismatched bodies.

"Let's go for a spin, see the underside of your city," he said.

He leaned forward to kiss me, but his lips were flaking, and I didn't want to taste them. His dry kiss stung, felt hard and easy, felt like landing on the moon. And there was movement on top of my ankle bones, like new bug bites, begging me to scratch.

Copenhagen

It's movie night at her place: Planet of the Apes. I'm not excited.

Elena has outdone herself: lasagne with lowfat cheese for my hubby and me. I'm on a diet and Elena thinks about other people that way, shopping for low fat cheese so I'll feel less guilty. It smells like garlic in her kitchen, home-like in a way my house never does.

***

Why don't I like Planet of the Apes? I hate it. I should have brought popcorn. Popcorn can really help.

Elena's mean little Juliette runs up to greet us. A dark silky-haired goddess who bites. We don't ever pet her. My husband says, "Juliette looks wonderful. Did you take her to Perfect Paws?"

I imagine him dancing with Juliette, letting himself be mauled.

Hubby and I—we are "happy" this week. I'm holding his hand, milking his fingers. He's pretending to be in love with me so that I'll stop moping. I told him I would leave. Now he tries.

***

When I can't sleep and he's away, Elena opens the door, smiling her garlicky grin. Somehow she reminds me of Danny Kaye in that Hans Christian Andersen movie. I can't remember the title, but it's full of swans and Copenhagen. Elena's smile is the world of ancient movies, the ones my mother loved.

"That Danny Kaye," Mom would say. "I wish men were really like that."

I enter Elena's house with no movies on queue. I sit next to her and smell garlic on her apron, her breath, her life. Juliette bites my finger, blood beads up like spilled wine. I forgive her for being a dangerous animal.

Alone, we don't need lowfat cheese. I pretend my husband approves of me being over here without him, since he's not in love with me anyway. "You look like a female Hans Christian Andersen," I say, kissing Elena's Scandinavian lips.

The Insides of Shells

The fat dog and I sat near the window. The window was covered with dust, the whole house was covered with dust and mold and sadness. I said to the dog that I had slept all morning again. He stood up for a bit, as if to place himself at the front of this impossible conversation.

He had not been my dog in the way that I had expected him to be my dog. Being overweight, and loving, and frightened of other dogs, he could easily be everything to me.

Should we go outside, Boy? I asked. We stayed there, trying to decide. I looked at him, he looked at me, and we thought about it.

By the time it became dark I felt as if the sea was closer than it really was. I actually heard it. It sounded like the way it used to sound when trying to listen to the insides of shells.

Fire Opal

He used to hide his arms when they first went out. Said their thick dark hair made him look simian. Now he acted proud of it, as if he could get away with things, the baby in her belly making him arrogant. He was too good looking, too crazy, her mother said. Nobody would believe she had gotten into this.

"Can't you even see one step ahead?" she thought. She went to him, pressing her hands underneath his shirt. When he picked her up, she felt like a doll, her swollen body light again.

"Take it back," she said.

He placed her on the sofa, covered her up with the blanket. He took the ring from her, set it on the coffee table.

Enjoy the beauty of it one last time, she thought. *Spend some time with it before he returns it to whoever he stole it from.*

Closing her eyes, she imagined the sun on her belly. She had never been to Mexico, so she locked her eyes on the Mexican Fire Opal, a fiery beauty surrounded by six garnets, little flecks of blood.

"Who deserves it more?" he said.

She felt water leaking from her eyes. It was even more beautiful out of focus.

And there was a new way he made love to her, something she hadn't known she would like, but did. She watched the colors and relaxed while he did it, taking his time. She locked her eyes, the light inside herself, the light inside the opal. It heated up, and the sun came out, swallowing the weaker colors.

Death Row Mouse

I bring my man a pet, a death-row mouse, nabbed from Rosie the albino python's lunch cage. At the Vivarium, nobody's standing near the doomed mice, so it's easy to do. I've learned a lot from hanging out there, watching the happy families slip in to see the snakes.

What's trickiest is trying to decide which mouse to save.

When I pluck one up by the tail, it flips around ungratefully, bites my fingertip, drawing blood. I slip out of the shop, a bleeding mouse-napper.

The manager squeaks, running out the door, waving his finger at me. I get on my bike with the white baby mouse in my zipper pocket, my ticket back into the man's life.

I explain this to him. *It's like being God*, I say.

Rain

Mr. Anderson and I understand each other. One thing we agree on: his wife is wonderful.

"She kicks me out of bed these days," he says. We laugh. "I really don't blame her," I say. We stand there looking at each other's profiles, waiting for something to happen.

I sleep in their living room, listening to the confusing rain. Mr Anderson sleeps with four pillows. His blonde handlebar mustache glows in the dark.

"Which part of dear Mr. Anderson do you like best?" I ask his wife. "Let's each take one side, and pull, and see what gives," she says.

Hiding Places

At my sister's memorial service, the men trickled in as if spit out by a toxic wave. Each more sad-looking than the one before. One of them planted himself near the egg sandwiches fingering the cherry pie, ignoring our serving tongs, threatening to make the rest of us sick. But he smelled gorgeous, like female-bait, handed me two black and white photos of my sister laying on a grassy hill next to Chuckles, her old dog.

"Thanks," I said, "should I know you?"

In the photos June looked so beautiful, hiding from everyone in the world, smiling up from the past, calling me Chicken-head. I tried not to laugh, because she always tickled me after she said it, her fingers around my waist, poking me so quickly I'd wet myself. "June let me take her photo," he said, "because she had no interest in fucking me." He seemed like a man ringed with sharp, genuine observations.

"My sister was in crisis," I said, as if this were news to anyone in the world. He looked a bit like June, this one, hiding behind weeds. I smiled up at him, showing off my wrinkle-free neck. And he smiled right back at me as if he were June in the grass, as if he could see past my hiding places.

Hand Clasp

Jane said it was his gentleness that hooked her. Mine have not been gentle, I said.

I was tired of hearing about Jane's opera of love. The way her guy brought her roses. "It isn't just the gentleness, it's his hand-clasp," she said. Jane and I were sixty years old, and I couldn't imagine any of this. How did she even meet him?

I stared at her skinny wrists, bleached-out hair. I imagined both of my exes trying to clasp, not grab, my hand, and it made me laugh.

What's funny? Jane asked.

"Nothing," I said. "There was that note, oh... just last Thursday," Jane said, pushing her point. "He gave me a yellow rose that day". It was almost Valentine's Day.

I fished around in my pockets, found them bulging with the promise of cigarettes.

"Smoke?" I said.

"Sure".

She took a cigarette from my hand-clasp. That's the way that it goes, I told myself, sucking on a serious taste, poisoning my air, wandering in the direction of my therapist's office. She was living in her fantasies, of course. Who knew what was true? Mostly these days she was white as a sheet. The fat had gone out of her smile.

Bingo

I fell for a clown called Bingo. I guess he loved me back. His fingers made me friendly. I had no interest in moving on to other parts. My toes made him happy. Too happy.

But, what happened was, he'd bite.

"Love nibbles," he call them. It would hurt, and I'd cry, but I never let him know how much I needed those bites. How he looked like my father. My father died when I was four years old.

"You're the prettiest gymnast I've ever known," Bingo said. But I wasn't happy about things. I wasn't a gymnast. My job was riding the zebra, doing flips on her back. Who did he think I was? What was he thinking would happen to me?

Eventually, I left the circus.

Sometimes I dream of him. The dreams are warm. I burrow into his body like I don't care about having a normal life. Love him the way a clown deserves to be loved.

I'm home, I say.

My Lover's Wife

My lover tells me about his wife's new outfit, her artful friends, her zippy vocabulary.

"Her word this week is 'Hiraeth'" he says.

"Intimidating."

"She is," he says. "God love her, but she's wonderful."

He sits there beaming about it while I unbutton his shirt and pull him out of his jeans. I ask him to describe her nightwear.

"Two piece, or the nightshirts?"

"Tell me about the past," I say. I ask him for more vital information each time. I treat him well because I value his visits.

"Well, he says, "when we were first married, oddly, there were the button-up flannel nightgown numbers. I called them passion-killers," he giggles.

"Yes, of course!"

I'm on the rug now, doing my naked stretches, stretching out my toes like worms, moving into the Downward Dog pose.

"But really, they're lovely memories, those early days," he says. "She was already like an old, familiar song."

"Lovely," I say, feeling the air on my ass.

"What is her favorite color?"

"I should know this," he says. "I'd say, aquamarine."

This makes me unaccountably happy. "Hey, that was my mother's favorite color too!"

"I don't know, I don't really want to know," he says.

I straddle him facing away. We do the reverse cowgirl thing. He's John Wayne on a horse while I'm facing my mint-green wall.

"Yee haw!" I shout, to add to the fun. But he's quiet, in the saddle. Pushing, but quiet.

I think about horses, about cowboys and cowgirls, and about the long career of John Wayne. How the new True Grit movie just couldn't live up to the old. The originals were so much better than remakes, is what I'm thinking when he finishes.

"Love ya, Duke," I say.

My lover has a shopping list, and he pulls it out of his brief case. He looks it over. Tells me he has to stop at the store before heading home. He shows it to me, it's her handwriting. Neat looking print, letters made with green ink.

"I'm jealous"! I say. "Looks like she's cooking up some black bean chili."

"I'm seriously lucky," he says, brushing some of my hair from his jeans. I walk him to the door for a goodbye hug.

"I do sometimes wish you could stay," I say, thinking of the quiet moments to come.

He smiles, and nods. "Me too, little Honey". I'm remembering my father right before he left us to live with his mistress. After each visit, I go over the reasons my father might have loved my mother.

Angela Readman

What Gorillas Do at Night

Contents

The Honey Gatherers

Whenever he touches me, I think of honey. The slick drip of it silking his hands. I let his fingers flow over me. Sunlight coats my tongue and glues pleasantries into my mouth. I lick off the sticky urge to complain about the state he's left the bathroom in and tell him to drive safe. If he forgets to say he loves me, it's OK. I'm collecting pollen from the flowers he doesn't buy, weeping it into my hive.

The supermarkets taught us how to love with those plastic cards, points granting the faithful rewards. I am a Honey, finally, a Sugar Babe, the app tells me. I message just the right amount of ☺ and xxxs. Not so many it would make him sigh, not so few he doesn't think anyone cares. I don't make a fuss about anything. It makes too much pop up. ☹ *You are not a honey. This is a guilt trip, a question, a need.* I'm relegated to drone.

Some girls wing it, fly out on a storm, tell a guy to shove it where the sun doesn't shine. It's not worth it, losing the honey. One wrong word could cost me so many points I'll only be able to love someone unthinkable next time, someone not signed to the scheme. Those who haven't got a single smiley heart or loyalty point to their name.

Honestly, it would be crazy. There'd be no way of knowing if they've earned a honey like me. That kind of love is a waggle dance in the dark.

In bed, we lie back to back, bottoms nudging. I hum my boyfriend goodnight and imagine bees collecting pollen to last the winter. Come spring, I'll have enough loyalty points to leave. And he'll have no choice but to bumble through life, a solitary worker buzzing around collecting any bit of sugar he can find.

Miss Monroe's Body Double on Something's Got to Give

One August, I was the shadow of a star. I wore capri pants and men angled lamps. It was like stuffing sunlight under my skin. I saw photos of you skinny dipping and paddled in the same pool. My shadow was yours. I slipped out of myself and into its silk. Whenever I moved, people thought of you.

I'd been dating a mechanic for years, but something switched. I held his interest in your fist. Men lit my cigarettes, fingers silvered by grazing your breasts in newsprint. So many small stones stitched to gauze, blinking like hail on fresh laundry.

I accepted every soda they offered me. I brushed against a cameraman's fingers and wondered if a president's feel the same. Some days I pretended the cola was champagne, a zillion meteors in my mouth. Others, I bet you imagined your champagne was milkshake.

That summer, I felt it too, a sort of burning, black holes in my belly. Someone would wait for me smile and sigh an ocean on their face, and I'd feel a weight.

I was a woman walking into her house discovering the dog she left behind woke at her scent. I was a figure at a poolside observing her babies learning to swim.

I strolled along the platinum streets after work, the wig a snowstorm balanced on my skull, my silhouette a trophy awarded to slightly disappointed men.

I walked by and felt their eyes flick through me, a calendar of dreams, so long as I didn't turn around.

The Day it Really Rained Men

It wasn't like you think the morning it rained men. They didn't arrive wearing gold shorts, perfectly muscular and fully formed. No one danced in the street. They couldn't dance at all. They were so small and naked. Shivering, they clung to the windows of the train.

It was drizzly, rain freckled my coat. The lady sitting opposite me spotted it first. Folding her plastic headscarf, she explained she didn't have her glasses with her and asked, 'What's this…?' She held out a palm to show me the rain.

I leaned so close I could smell the lint in her pockets. The rain wasn't clear. It was silvery, brown, golden, and pink. Each drop was different. Each was a man. Some sat on our shoulders. Some pooled into clusters, some rolled down our arms like children sledging on a hill

'It's men,' I said.

'About time.' The lady unbuttoned her coat and splashed a handful of rain down the front of her blouse.

Other passengers were starting to notice now. The carriage shuffled, women squinting. One little girl shook an umbrella over her mother's bag, determined to carry as much of the rain as she could.

'Look, teeny men! If we take one home and feed him maybe he'll grow.'

There were plenty of us who did the same. We collected the rain in bottles and jars. We moved the jars around our windowsills and dropped in scraps of pizza, lasagne, wine and beer, but the rain remained the same size whatever we did.

We lay in our bathtubs and felt it pour over us, a thousand chests too small to bury our heads in, arms that could never hold us.

Two Girls Contemplate What Gorillas Do at Night

They stand outside the enclosure, just like last Thursday. Ever since her father won passes at work, Neko drags May to the zoo after school. It would be a waste not to. The frozen yogurt stand's closed. They observe the gorilla without sprinkles.

Kyoto sits on a rock, knuckles under his chin. *Thinking.* People point. Children laugh, their voices sharpened by seeing animals do anything.

Neko brushes dust off her kilt and knots her fingers. Kyoto flexes his biceps. May grabs her camera. There are a hundred pictures on her memory now, but none look like standing here feels.

The afternoon sun circles the cage and picks through fur. The girls think it looks like someone looking for a lost silver chain.

***

May walks home, fingertips pattering her satchel. She missed piano practise, but she got a decent photo of

Kyoto for her art portfolio. Neko's never into that stuff anymore; she has a boyfriend instead. He gave her a keyring shaped like a tortoise. It's probably love.

It'll be dark soon, a pelt of frost settles on the lawn, creaking under her feet.

The kitchen is steamy, May's mother stands by the sink draining pasta. She dyed her hair a week ago, but one grey strand already springs from her crown.

'Do you like the eggplant?' she asks her new boyfriend, fiddling with her freshly blonde hair.

'I do,' he says. His oily mouth is full.

May chews in silence, wondering what gorillas do at night. The silver on his back looked like unravelled moonlight.

***

It's only soap, but Neko pretends its perfume when Lars nuzzles her neck. He must do it quietly. Officially, he's already left; her parents are in bed.

They've already done it twice, but this time he looks at her while he's inside and asks if she's close. She tells him she is. She feels close to something but isn't sure what it is.

Lars comes, zips his flies, kisses her another goodbye and goes.

Neko closes the door and picks up the winter gloves he left on the counter. Kyoto's palms looked similar, like, if that gorilla got the chance, he could drive anywhere.

She puts on a glove and runs a leather finger across her cheek. It's her favourite part of the evening, the perfection of absence moving over her skin, imagining.

Learning to Speak Dolphin

You can't blow up a balloon without seeing the dolphins you worked with that summer. A dropped can of jalapenos broke your foot, and every morning you slipped off one shoe by the pool. The work was simple: socialise with the dolphins, jiggle buckets of mackerel, fish heads slapping against steel.

Their owner was researching communication. He wanted to know, if you speak to a dolphin enough, will it understand? It was important to speak carefully and fill each word with praise. The knack to it was to picture each word was a flower opening in your mouth. After a while, your boss made you wear lipstick so he could see every shape you made.

You didn't fuck him, though you slept with everyone else. Your friends left for dance school and sex became your new ballet. After, you'd lie back and tell your latest boyfriend all about the dolphins. Those funny faces they made in front of the mirror in the pool. They swam against it, rubbing algae off the glass with their bodies to see themselves better. The boyfriends interpreted this as meaning you wanted to go again. This time on your knees.

You didn't expect anything when you got a job at the café. Learning the language of dolphins was over. The funding dried up. You didn't think about it much. Standing on a chair, you cleaned a fog of grease off the windows while some older guy watched. He told you the way you reached up with a soapy cloth reminded of him of Swan Lake.

You married him and quit work ASAP. He has enough for both of you, he says. He means money, but you know he means love. His kids keep having birthdays and parties, it's that sort of house. They scoff cake and run into the sprinkler squealing before they hurl.

You kiss their foreheads, dip their sticky balloons into the paddling pool and picture dolphins. Swimming to the lip of the pool, rising in the water to greet you each morning. You understood the smiles boned to their faces, the gleeful sounds they made. They didn't know how to do anything else. Everyone would be able to speak dolphin, you're sure, if they'd given it longer. The experiment ended too soon.

Girly

Maybe it's because I wore nothing but gingham until I was eleven. Or, because I'd still grind with my girlfriends in hot pants and bralettes, like Pollyanna gone feral. Maybe it's because all my baby teeth dropped out at six. (I kissed *everyone*.) Or it's the Jawbreakers I licked until they painted my lips with the lipstick I wasn't allowed. Or it's because our curtains stayed closed a whole summer. Maybe it's because I snuck out and stole the orange juice next door. Maybe it's because my sister's shoe looked so lonely, a lovely kitten heel. Maybe it's because she was Supergirl every chance she got and was prettier than she knew. Maybe some people feel too alive to ever fear walking alone. Maybe a smile isn't always a smile. Maybe it's because my mother froze when a zombie cheerleader knocked at our door. Or how I shepherded her inside, still in costume, my Lisa Simpson cheek making hers jaundiced. Maybe it's because having your birthday on Halloween sounds the bomb, until you realise all your cakes will be coffins. Maybe it's because biology killed me. And I hated sitting near that kid who kept drawing anatomically correct vaginas on his notebook. Or it's because I got my period once in gymnastics. Maybe its cruel all shorts aren't black. Maybe Ethan heard about that and felt sad. Maybe because his mother left, and the house got so lousy some kid pinned him down once and wrote UNCLEAN on his forehead.

Maybe Magic Markers are everything that's wrong with society. Maybe it's because he's 5ft tall and no one else said yes. Or, because when I look in the mirror, I still see gingham. Maybe I can't live another day looking like an outline on the pavement. Maybe I watch too much Disney, and when they found that shoe on the street where my sister was last seen, for a second, I thought Cinderella. Maybe I'm a sucker for bottled beer and playing who'd we Fuck, Marry or Kill…? under a moon like Fanta. Maybe it just felt right. Felt so good someone froze the documentary forever playing in my head. Maybe it was dumb, and I don't care. I let him. Let myself. Ever since I've stroking my stomach, whispering *Girly, Girl…*

Sleeping with Our Eyes Open

The perfect guy arrived at my door. I knew he was perfect because he said so. Just like my husband used to say he *knows me*. It was -10, but he showed up in shorts. I say shorts because the word Speedo makes me picture people pissing in swimming pools, but that's what he was wearing.

'Can I help you?' I flicked on the porchlight. That's when he told me, shivering and smiling like Miss Alaska. He wasn't wearing a shirt and his nipples reminded me of my first lipstick. It was called *Candygirl.* Rosy as a prom date slap.

'I've brought you something.' He handed me a plastic bag with Tinkerbell on the front. I had one the same at fourteen. I kept cigarettes, gum, and a black bra inside. Opening it, I found they were still there. Along with tulips, crusty bread, wine, and every Valentine's card I imagined receiving between the age of five and thirty-six.

I stared at the snowflakes latching onto his eyelashes. He wiped his face and I saw two fingers were missing.

Another was unusually long, spatula-esque. I thought of G I Joe, the rubber fingers I'd gnawed before moving him into Barbie's shoebox apartment.

'I've moved on,' I said, 'seriously. I'm sorry.'

The guy started walking away. His fuzzy hair looked like flock wallpaper. The snow whipping against him, he started humming a Smith's song and I called, 'Wait…'

He turned, a scar on one cheek like he'd had to fight for something. I wanted him to say something to prove he was the perfect man, but I didn't know what. I figured he'd have been carrying cash, or a kitten. Or something. The loaf he brought smelt fresh. I'd take it over chocolates any day. The flowers were purple.

'I don't know where to put you,' I said, 'I don't have space.'

He followed me indoors making himself smaller with each step. Small enough to squeeze into the cupboard with the vacuum cleaner. He showed me how he could shrink to fit in. And slip out whenever I wanted, no worse for it.

I poured wine, tore into the bread and sat on the kitchen

floor. He sat opposite, backs to the cupboards. Occasionally, I heard something in the lounge, my husband browsing his computer, spilling a beer. I didn't get up. I noticed the lino needed polishing and stretched out my legs.

'I forgot how it feels to just sit anywhere,' I said, 'I hate chairs.'

The perfect guy squeezed my foot. Let it rest on his thigh. I looked at him. He looked at me. Late into the night, we sat that way drinking. Close as dolls laid side by side in their shoebox apartment, sleeping with their eyes open.

Procedures for the Detective after Thelma & Louise

You can't stand on the brink of that canyon forever. The freeze frame dissolves into slush, even if want to hold those women in sunglasses flying forever. You want to see only sky, sky, sky, sky like four TV's in their eyes. You can't. Don't look down.

Listen to your colleagues at the station. Complaints about women and paperwork. Damn waste of a classic car. The cowboy who stole Thelma's money is on bail. Keep thinking of the way he made humping gestures on his way to the door. Forever fucking an invisible girl.

You will want to buy flowers coming home, can't say why. Your wife sniffs with suspicion or gratitude. Be unsure. Think of a husband whose wife is gone scraping pizza off his sandals. Attend the sink after supper, wash the plates. You can do more.

Drive by that house again. Look through the windows- the room as the dead woman left it. Embroidered roses dangling on the dishcloth. Lace curtains breathing butterflies onto another day so hot the golf course fries. Slot your Visa in the door, sit where she sat for a while.

Look at the photo of that child with the baton. That twirler, all skinny hopes and dreams. The picture is labelled *Louise. Thirteen. Trials.* Wonder what she tried for, why it mattered, if she kept trying. Wonder more.

Kiss your wife's neck tonight at the stove. Take the pan from her hand. Touch that photograph, swirl it in your pocket. Keep twirling. Twirl for your life.

Cowgirls

I became a cowboy, though I'd never rode a horse in my life. I looked at my feet and saw the boots poking out of my bed sheets. It felt right. I'd had a voice like starlight stuck in my throat. Whenever I said something pretty, it sounded like it hurt.

I phoned my cousin and swapped my buzzcut Sindy for his spurs. He told me I wasn't a cowboy, and besides, it would be a *cowgirl.* I didn't need anyone to tell me what I was. I knew. The sky glowed. The chemical works flared one last time, and I heard a river inside me.

I walked along the street in my spurs, steel scraping haloes all over the concrete. The world was my cigar. I kicked sparks. Kids laughed, wheeling past on their bikes. I gave them the Eastwood stare and swished my poncho of air.

Everyone laughed, except certain girls. Girls who needed a cowboy sometimes for their games.

'My mother's crazy', Amy said, pretending a bull got loose outside Esso's. Not in a way that left bruises, just in a way that involved falling in love every few months.

'I can't like the guys anymore,' she said, 'if I do, poof! He disappears.'

I offered her my silence like a pool of fresh rain where a calf could graze and see its face. I held out my hand and she stroked it, it's map of somewhere other than here.

'My sister has so many jobs, she gets up and cleans in her sleep like we're living in a dirty hotel,' Tina told me at the school gate. I described Montana in winter, foals being dragged into nights like wet silk, lassos looped around the moon. The days got away.

Sometimes, I swore, for Sunday school sorts. When Lisa's brother didn't return from the army, and Mary's father got laid off and burnt cables for copper. I cunted and pissered, doodled sunglasses on Jesus, and offered my face to slap.

It sounded like a snapped reign, they said, holding what they'd been told nice girls should say. I carried those smacks like kidskin gloves and lifted my hat. I saw they were dying to try it on.

Mr Travolta Stops Dancing

I opened my eyes and found my ex had brought John Travolta over. He stood in my lounge chuckling, my ex, not Mr Travolta.

We split up years ago but found ourselves sharing an apartment last year, in-between someone to love and share rent. These days, he popped in to talk wedding plans and bring free shit from work. Last time, it was 5 litres of Christmas Pudding ice-cream. Today, John. Cardboard, life-size and sticky with popcorn caresses.

'Can you believe someone left him near the dumpster?' he said, 'I rescued him for you, I remembered you like him.'

I looked at the guy. Brow wrinkled where the weather got to him. He wore a black suit and looked puzzled.

'I loved him when I was a kid,' I said. Grease John, Saturday Night Fever John. Not at the disco, more when he was at work selling paint and only pictured himself dancing.

'You want me to take him?' my ex asked, 'if you don't like it…' I looked at him, plumped by lasagne and photos of flower arrangements his fiancé kept feeding him. I'd never laughed with anyone as much as this guy. Never faked as much either.

'No,' I said, 'Mr Travolta can stay.'

My ex smiled like a childhood picture I once saw. We did that, shared our baby photos like auditions for all the babies we'd have. He'd been dressed as a little newsreader, face peering out of a television box. Later, he discovered his father crashed his car. He always said it felt worse to find out like that, dressed so smart in his suit.

'Lamb or chicken?' he asked, shoulder touching Travolta like a best man.

'Lamb. People forget chicken. Even when it's good, it's just chicken.'

'That's what I keep saying.' He gave John a high-five and left, rehearsing another night full of menus.

I moved John by the window. He stood there, hands in the air. I dressed for bed and draped my bra over his fingers. Let it dangle. The figure lived there for years. From outside, it resembled a lover dressed for dinner, perpetually wandering through my house. Looking to find me waiting for something.

Shit to Do with a Wedding Dress

1. Take pictures (irreverent is best.) Free the formal wear to be a bath towel, scratch the odd ball. Drop it on a wet floor. You will bring this dress to its knees.

2. White is a problem, makes you blind. Think kitchens: duster, tablecloth, the lace cuff is a doily under your can. Watch the dog circle and lie on the floor. Open another beer. Sit by the dog.

3. Take it out. Now. Feel the weight of silk in your arms. It's windy, carry the dress to the garage like bearing the burden of a loose woman too drunk to dance. Toss it on the Harley, rub the leather seat till it shines. Remember no woman's behind.

4. Did you take it far enough? Tonight the dress is back, flopped out on the grass outside. Kick it. Don't apologise.

5. The skirt fits the birdcage just fine. Every day you expect to find a dead canary, morning trills, unbearably beautiful and yellow when you lift the net.

6. Use it however you can. Tie up the ends, string the skirt between trees. The dress is a hammock. You think you're too heavy, imagine getting cozy then hearing satin split, pushing you out to the ground like something still born.

7. Make a scarecrow. Try different Halloween masks. Darth Vader. Yoda. Cher. Notice the dress suits all and none. Look out the window, see its face lift in the wind.

8. Bring it in. Don't know why. The fabric's grey, brocaded in fox piss, jewelled by rain. Pigeons have pinned a lily-white corsage to its breast. Give the dress room to dry out on its back. Starch it. Firm. Leave your drink and crawl under the skirt. It's an igloo, so cool, a man could live here.

9. The dress tells many jokes. Laugh.

10. Tell your friends everything you did, all the piss, spills and shit, but not how long you stayed in the igloo. Everything looks paler from the inside. You close your eyes and sleep in it. It's like waking to find snow deeper than its been for a while.

Fresh

Zoe always brings the salad. Jack loves watching her peel. Never wasting lettuce, scratching a calf with one foot. Her wet hands full of dark leafy greens like she's trying to hold onto a kiss in the rain. Those sandals she wears have seen better days, but they'll do. It's refreshing to meet a frugal woman.

Later, she'll unbutton her shirt and flop into that scruffy sweater she can't throw away. He thinks this bodes well for him. Those holes in the sleeves she loops over her fingers like gloves. It's adorable. Of course, they'll make love, but first there's always salad.

Dressing, pepper, anecdotes about work. She teaches sex ed and, hearing her tell it, no two students blush the same shade of red. Jack laughs. She rakes through lettuce and jabs a crescent moon on her fork. All day it has been a penis, that cucumber. He's pretty sure he could marry her, if it wasn't for that. The crunch of staring at her pretty teeth, thinking *Penis, penis, penis.*

Wild Geese

I was in her kitchen when Chloe told me she never broke wind in front of her husband. The sun slanting in, a slice of lemon floating in her cup.

Throughout her marriage, whenever she had to go to the bathroom, she cleaned the whole thing like an alibi, she admitted. This is what we do in the interests of romance.

Two years after her death, she's still romantic. I sit with her husband at the table he painted *Sorbet* and wish I'd brought lemons. He's still hot. I am still single. I'd never tell anyone what his wife told me. Girl-code.

Nothing's been the same, he says, since her death. The house is so quiet he knows it misses her. Even the doors express grief. They no longer creak. The floorboards sympathise by holding their silence.

The day is still. The sky is the colour of a Tiffany's box that has sat in a sunroom for too long. He runs his hand through his hair, looks out the window and says, whatever happened to all the wild geese?

The Night Life of Wives

Every night I let strangers into the house when my husband is in bed. I ease the latch open, aware of the click. Lips pursed, I raise a finger and usher people into the hall. I know nothing about anyone, other than their clothes.

One girl is hardly out of her teens. She wears fleecy fabrics and a hat with kitty ears, prepared for cold weather or a sleepover. It could go either way.

Another regular looks like a banker who's lost his briefcase.

Whoever they are, they slip into stocking feet and congregate by the stairs, small flashlights and candles cradled in their hands.

'You can go up now,' I say, 'follow me. Shsh...' They follow me past the still row of their shoes, a line of people making hush sounds soft as damp fingers putting a candle to rest. Outside the bedroom, we release our whispers and bow our heads.

The air is full of my husband's breathing. We tip toe in adjusting our heartbeats, each person learns to breathe in when he does. Breathe out.

'He looks so calm,' one girl whispers. 'Content,' the banker agrees.

They sit on the floor crossed legged, tea-lights by their knees. They watch the man keep his eyes closed, frozen, aware our slightest move could break something.

Some nights, he turns his head or drapes one arm over the duvet, and we gasp. Others, he flings off the covers, murmurs something we can't understand and returns the silence to us.

'Do you think he was trying to say something?' a woman in satin whispers, her dress is uncertain whether she's on her way to a party or coming back.

'I don't think so. We shouldn't put words into still mouths,' says an overall man, 'He sleeps. That's all we need to know.'

In flickering darkness, we try to understand nothing and allow someone's sleep to wash over us, comforting as a strip of light under a door. I rush no one. It's like dipping into sunlit water when your hands are always cold, one woman admits on the stairs. It's like being accepted, another man claims.

One by one, the visitors leave once they've had their fill. They shake my hand and thank me; some hug me so close I can't move.

It is neither night nor true morning. The sky looks like a chalkboard wiped clear of yesterdays. Only the faintest wisps of words remain. I stand on my doorstep and watch strangers wander along my street in bare feet. Rain on their soles, they sidestep broken glass on the path and wander out of sight. Quietly, I let myself into the house, just about able to drift off myself.

Jeff Alessandrelli

The Days of Wine & Roses;

or An Orphan's Tale

Aristotle. Andrew Jackson.
Billie Holiday. Joseph Smith.
Cinderella. Punky Brewster. Ice-T.
Marilyn Monroe. Elizabeth Bishop.

Leo Tolstoy. Tina Turner.
John Keats. Malcolm X.
Ella Fitzgerald. J.R.R. Tolkien.
William Wordsworth. Pollyanna.

Nelson Mandela. Tarzan.
Joseph Conrad. Ray Charles.
James Bond. Snow White.
Moses. Muhammad. Babe Ruth.

Eleanor Roosevelt. Edgar
Allen Poe. Louis Armstrong.
Tallulah Bankhead. Johann Sebastian Bach.
Little Annie, Little Orphan Annie.

Years of shaping your idea
of a mother out of a hot meal
cooked over a low fire,
the starlight blindingly bright

behind you. So water sweats
through the dank dark walls
of the dirty old towns.
Is it better to be deceived

by luminous shadows or luminous flesh
is a question any orphan
might ask. & no matter the destination,
it's easy to outgrow a map.

The days of wine & roses.
There is much uncertainty
beneath the weight
of the starlight's moon.

In the dirty crevices of an orphan's history
centuries of wrath & night.
Fresh as a daisy in a brand-
new hybrid, Oliver Twist

was a fraud, a fiction.
A primmed up glam
act of glitter & mirth.
If it is true

that we live
in an age of experiment
then every morning more blood
should rush out the spout.

Later, dusk. The light
puts on a pair of dark shoes
&, starstruck, soaks its feet in the lonely river.
Time. Doubt.

Whether spoken out loud or written
down & over & down & down & over again,
time is the most used noun in the English language.
I'm a different person now an orphan says

to herself & opens the refrigerator door to stare
into the sunset, the dirty,
cluttered remnants of a sunset
that was once some strictly regimented tableau.

How long has that been in there? How old is that?
What's in that? How old is that? How—
Accumulation is a reason for &
understanding of disorder.

Too many jars & bottles
unidentifiable, vague plastic containers,
fresh vegetables, wilted wilting tinfoil, red red meat.
Time. Time. Time. Time. Time. Time. Time. Time.

Every bridge is born
wearing braces, impeccably placed headgear
that fits just tight. The mouth
of the river is straightened

by the machinery of land.
From the dirty plexi-glass of a passing train,
passing train crossing a dirty mountain,
a nameless orphan studies

the water's progress beneath. Steady
is a word to be used
only at a severe cost.
Chance spares us choice—

red wine, red roses, broken
secrets, impossible. A bridge is a metaphor
for nothing. It's easy to outgrow a map.
Blowing on the world's loneliness, a stuttering wind.

Why spend your whole life shivering under the tyranny of white snow?
she thinks to herself, throwing the black snowball as hard
as she can against the air,
watching it appear upward until it doesn't.

Utilizing instructions from a *Calvin and Hobbes* comic strip,
she'd spent all morning coalescing the dirt and bark,
the misshaped granules of ice & gravel. Task completed,
she then tried to rid herself of her creation
as quickly as possible.

(Orphanhood is a delicate proposition,
one of performing open-hearted brain surgery
on several patients simultaneously
while blindfolded, handcuffed.)

She studies her hands, wishes there were more useful callouses.
She peers in the direction of a darkness now absent, fallen.
Seeing a furled bouquet pawing at the back of her imagination's mind,
she gleefully considers how flowers are carnivores of light.

Entering history at the margins,
in the cracks, the too brightly-lit
or dimly-apprehended corners,
crannies, crawl-spaces.

What are beliefs well-honed & nurtured
except beliefs that will one day be
misremembered. Dozens of times
I've surfed the coast of Nebraska.

Dozens of times I've skied
the frigid slopes of Haiti
& Jamaica & sweltering
Ho Chi Minh City.

The flatness of the earth might
only be apprehended through
the universe's vast spherical shapelessness.
Belief's a plentiful act. Now   take it back.

What we have forsaken
can be realized
only by what
we have kept behind.

The world is my idea,
finely filigreed into separate compartments:
these walls of words are a sociality
brokering no closure, a see-through couture.

Life is a broken secret
impossible not to
twist & shout.
Fresh coffee with worm milk.

Death is an impossible secret.
The fabric of daylight will always fade,
night arriving & descending.
Spilt roses & stale wine.

A blind man brushing up against a dusty curtain
can always tell when it's morning,
sense when it's night,
while nevertheless remaining without sight.

I've never seen my mother's face.
She may have committed suicide
simply by holding her breath.
Spoken out loud certain words rot

an orphan's teeth, burn their tongues.
But a pair of dark red shoes,
dark & bright, are forever worth repeating.
When the docent describes the painting

to the blind man at the museum
he nods vigorously, sets a hand
on the docent's shoulder, says
"It's boring, my man. & I've already seen it."

Truth lies at the bottom of a well
an orphan once said
somewhere black & humble & quiet.
Later, in the early morning,

fate splashes everywhere
from the air. Peeking her head over
she spat into the deep
once, twice, thrice.

Wells give orphans
nothing to yell or shout about.
Nowhere to shout
when there's no distance

left to run, bottom's arrival
too dark to see.
It's easy to outgrow a map.
Time, time, pangs of time.

As a child black flowers lined the path
to the schoolyard. Gravity was a required
subject, expressed daily, but at recess
the swing set & the monkey bars

provided a tantalizing respite.
Years later I now realize that waking up & kissing a mirror
good morning is something millions of people do
without thinking twice,

but an orphan will only do so
under threat of violence.
Beneath both the deep-blue of the sky
& the sky-blue of the ocean,

who isn't a slave underwater? I've never
seen my mother's face. Isaac Newton,
the inventor of gravity, was an orphan.
Don't say of course.

How in the end every translator is a traitor
to the mother tongue.
How through language—words worse than
letters—
reading is a lie, a passing deceit.

How the little longness
of life is a lie, a deceit.
Great many broken secrets
impossible to twist & shout.

How the disturbing fact that
flesh flowers most fully in the summer,
the balmy spring.
Teal-blue tanktops & red bikinis & forest-green
bikinis.

Then *wild flowers out of gas*
everywhere at an orphan's feet
and how exacting lack
as a form of utterance is, can be.

A thief should be the keenest student of the law.
What proof then exists?
For reasons unclear
100% of all male orphans ejaculate

coagulated black sperm.
Everywhere they go they seem to find
harps impossible to play.
Lakes without shores.

What we thought were trucks
downshifting on the highway
was actually the sound of a meandering river
miles away an orphan slowly said

somewhere very quiet.
Dark muddy shores without lakes.
Pieces of an ignoble river
I've never seen.

Once an orphan found a desiccated human skull
in the dregs of a summer river
& used it as a water bowl for the abandoned dog
she'd found in the street, been secretly stowing.

So the days of wine & roses:
beneath a mountain of stars
we drink until we drown
& that's no way to end a party

celebrating someone else's birth.
Death is a balancing act,
dust the only tension keeping its wire
walkable, rigid, right in front.

It's too easy to force blood out of stones.
Time, pangs of—it's too easy.
Quick eternity, the waterfall's trickle
menaces with leisure. Fuck it.

Carefully writing with both right & left
hands skywriters make
pale canvases of the sky.
& the vowels fumed are red

blood cells, the consonants exhausted white,
both furiously vanishing to reach
the heart of the period of the end
of the sentence.

Life is special. But not like that.
This century's vast will be remembered
only for the work of its skywriters,
work written in the sky

& disappeared immediately.
In a family way, distended,
so we mirage steadily forward.
Spiteful, salvation-worn, we armor our hearts.

CODA

Abandoning a child is never having
to say you're sorry.
Choosing one's history orphans
the certainty of no choice.

& to think I once considered myself
the type of person that would sing
even if my throat was slit.
To think.

Biographies & Acknowledgments

Meg Pokrass is the author of six flash fiction collections and a two-time recipient of San Francisco's *Blue Light Book Award.* Her flash fiction has appeared in *Electric Literature, Wigleaf, McSweeney's,* and many literary journals. Her work has been widely internationally anthologized including 2 *Norton Anthology Readers* and *The Best Small Fictions.* She currently serves as Series Co-Editor for Best Microfiction and teaches flash fiction online.

Thanks to the following publications in which these stories previously appeared: An Object At Rest (*Ghost Parachute*); Worries of the Duck (*Cellulose Pajamas)*; Greetings from Mars (*KYSO Flash);* Copenhagen *(Funicular Magazine);* Rain, *(100 Word Story Magazine);* My Lover's Wife (*Connotation).*

Angela Readman's stories have won The Anton Chekov Award for Short Fiction, The Costa Short Story Award and The Mslexia Competition. Her collection *Don't Try This at Home* was short listed in The Edge Hill Prize and was the winner of The Rubery Book Award. In 2019 And Other Stories published her first novel, *Something like Breathing.* She lives in Northumberland.

Thanks to Meg Pokrass for her encouragement and to the publishers that published some of these pieces separately: Girly—I'll Show Your Mine Winner (*Sex Writing Journal, the Publishing Project 2019*), Shit to Do with a Wedding Dress *(Smokelong Quarterly);* The Honey Gatherers *(Great Jones Street);* The Night Life of Wives (Great Jones Street & Sleep is a Beautiful Colour *(The National Flash Fiction Day Anthology, Gumbo);* Sleeping with Our Eyes Open *(And We Pass Through (the National Flash Fiction Day Press);* Learning to Speak Dolphin *(The Short Story Flash 400);* Two Girls Contemplate What Gorillas Do at Night *(New Flash Fiction Review).*

Jeff Alessandrelli is the author of the poetry collections *THIS LAST TIME WILL BE THE FIRST* (2014) and *Fur Not Light* (2019), both from Burnside Review Press. He's also the author of a hybrid poetic biography, published by Ravenna in 2011, of the French avant-garde composer Erik Satie entitled *Erik Satie Watusies His Way Into Sound.* Based in Portland, OR, in addition to his own writing Alessandrelli also runs the literary record label/press Fonograf Editions. He may be found at https://jeffalessandrelli.net.

Portions of *The Days of Wine & Roses; or An Orphan's Tale* were originally published at The Portland Review and Coconut. Thank you to the editors.